TABLE OF CONTENTS

Tiger tees off at the 2002 Masters.

GOLF MASTER

Tiger Woods stood at the 18th tee and took a golf club from his bag. It was his **driver**, his biggest club. Fans cheered and shouted, "Attaway, Tiger! You go T!" Tiger grinned and **teed up** his golf ball. Then he smacked the ball far into the sky. It landed in the **fairway**—a perfect shot.

Tiger was playing the final hole of the 2002 Masters Tournament. The Masters is the first of four important golf events—called **majors**—played every year.

Tiger takes the long walk up the 18th fairway with Retief Goosen. Tiger and Retief were playing together.

Tiger was leading the tournament by three **strokes**. If he could keep the lead, he would win the Masters for the third time. Only two golfers have ever won the famous tournament more times. But no one had ever won so many times at such a young age. Tiger was still just twenty-six years old.

Jack Nicklaus won the Masters six times. Arnold Palmer won the tournament four times. They are the only golfers who have won the Masters more times than Tiger.

Tiger hit his second shot from the fairway. The ball arched through the sky like a rainbow and landed on the **green**. The crowd stood and cheered as Tiger walked to the green. Tiger smiled and waved and tipped his cap. He **putted** the ball close to the hole. Then he calmly tapped it into the cup to win the great tournament yet again.

Each time a golfer wins the Masters, he is given a green jacket to wear. Tiger got his third green jacket in 2002.

Tiger's big grin shows how much he enjoyed golfing, even at less than two years old!

CUB WITH A CLUB

Eldrick Woods was born December 30, 1975, to Earl and Kultida Woods. His father called the baby "Tiger." This was the nickname of a

Vietnamese army officer and friend. In the 1970s, the original "Tiger" had saved Earl's life during the Vietnam War.

Young Tiger and his parents lived in Cypress, California. Earl got Tiger a small set of clubs when the boy was not yet two years old. Tiger rarely let go of his putter.

Before long, he was playing at his first golf course. On the first hole, it took him eleven strokes to put the ball in the hole. Soon he began appearing on national television shows to show off his special talent.

In 1977, when Tiger was not yet three, he appeared on *The Mike Douglas Show*. He hit a driver and putted with the famous comedian Bob Hope.

At age four, Tiger was taking golf seriously. He practiced driving the ball and putting.

Tiger practiced golf nearly every day. He whacked balls at the **driving range** and practiced on the **putting green**. At age six, he got his first **hole in one**.

Sometimes, while Tiger was swinging his club, his father would make noises on purpose. He was trying to help Tiger learn to concentrate on his game.

Other times, Tiger and his father played just

to have fun. They would hit the ball while standing on one foot or try to sink putts with their eyes closed.

When Tiger was eight, he began competing in golf tournaments. He played in his first Junior World Championship. This tournament was for boys who were ten years old and under. Tiger won!

When Tiger was six, his parents gave him a tape that played soft music with a voice that spoke messages. Some of the messages were "I focus and give it my all" and "I believe in me." Tiger played the tape over and over again while practicing his golf swing.

In 1984, Tiger lines up a putt at his first Junior World Tournament.

Tiger's real name is Eldrick. His parents, Earl and Kultida, put the first letter of each of their names on both ends of their son's name. They wanted to show him that they will always be at his side.

Soon he was playing and winning everywhere. At the age of eleven, he played in over thirty junior tournaments. He won them all.

Tiger's friends played Little League baseball. Tiger preferred golf. But Tiger was not allowed to play golf until he did his homework. His mother, Kultida, made sure of that. She was originally from Thailand, a country in Asia. Tiger felt very proud of his Asian background.

Earl and Tiger have a special bond. Earl's interest in golf sparked Tiger's.

LAUNCHING A CAREER

Tiger's life was a scramble. He traveled with his father to play in golf tournaments everywhere. Sometimes, his father drove all through the night. Other times, they flew in airplanes. Tiger won a tournament in Colorado. He won another in Florida. He won twice in Texas.

Tiger was a skinny kid, but he had a good swing by the time he was in high school.

When Tiger was fourteen, he had several coaches, together called Team Tiger. One coach was named Jay Brunza. He helped Tiger focus and relax during a match. As a freshman in high school, Tiger was the best golfer on the

In one tournament, Tiger hit a bad shot. Angry with himself, he smacked his club into his bag. Kultida saw him do it. She didn't approve of bad behavior. She reported his action to the officials and asked that Tiger lose two strokes.

school team. He was keeping up with his studies, too, and earned good grades.

In 1991, Tiger won the U.S. Junior **Amateur** Championship. He was the youngest winner ever. So many trophies filled his bedroom, he could barely get to his bed.

Tiger played in his first **professional** (pro)

Tiger first played against professional golfers at the 1992 Los Angeles Open.

tournament at the age of sixteen. Tiger was still an amateur. He was not a pro yet. This meant that Tiger could not earn **prize money**. But he could still compete against—and learn from—great professional golfers.

The event was the 1992 Los Angeles Open at Riviera Country Club. Tiger stood on the first tee and hit his shot down the fairway. With that, he had become the youngest person ever to play in an event sponsored by the **Professional Golfers' Association (PGA)**. He shot 72 that day and 75 the next. He **missed the cut** by six strokes.

In 1992, Tiger stood six feet tall, but he weighed just 140 pounds. Being thin as a pencil didn't help his golf game. He didn't have the strength to hit the ball long distances. He tried to gain weight any way he could. He ate two dinners. He ate midnight snacks. He lifted weights to get stronger. Eventually, he began to hit the ball farther.

Even though golf was a huge part of Tiger's life, he relaxed with friends. He especially enjoyed playing video games and Ping-Pong. He developed a love for fast food, too.

Tiger holds the trophy for having won his first U.S. Amateur Championship in 1994.

A SHOOTING STAR

Tiger continued to win tournaments and to get good grades. He earned a place at Stanford University in northern California. In his first year, he was the top college golfer in the country. That year he played in his first U.S. Amateur Championship. Tiger had to defeat one opponent each day to move on to the next round. He won every match. He trailed his final opponent by six strokes before rallying to win on the final hole. It was the greatest come-from-behind win in the history of the tournament.

Tiger finished high school with good grades. Colleges around the country offered him a free education if he would go to their school. Tiger's first choice was Stanford University in California.

In 1995, Tiger became the youngest player ever to compete in the Masters. He made the cut and finished with a four-day total of five over **par.**

The great golfer Nick Faldo *(seated)* watched as Tiger took a big swing at his first Masters tournament.

Tiger broke several college records and won the U.S. Amateur title twice more. He was ready to turn pro. On August 28, 1996, newspaper reporters and TV crews gathered to hear Tiger announce that he was joining the PGA Tour. Tiger leaned into a microphone and said two words: "Hello, world."

In 1996, Tiger won his third U.S. Amateur Championship in a row. His coaches and his dad *(second from right)* celebrate the victory. Tiger turned pro soon afterward.

The Nike "swoosh" is on Tiger's hats and shirts.

He signed **endorsement** deals with two companies—Nike and Titleist. Both make sports equipment. He would make commercials to advertise their sporting goods. In return, they would pay him a total of $60 million. Tiger was instantly rich.

Nearly all pro golfers are white. Tiger enjoys a mixture of ethnic backgrounds. From his father, he gets his African American, Native American, and white roots. From his mother comes his Asian background, partly Thai and partly Chinese. Tiger sees himself simply as an American. The endorsement companies saw Tiger's youth and background as a big plus in selling their products.

Kultida is often in the crowd during Tiger's matches.

THE GREATEST EVER

Tiger quickly got better while playing his first three pro tournaments. He finished 60th, then 11th, then 6th. Finally, at the Las Vegas Invitational in Nevada, Tiger won his first pro tournament. He was handed the winner's check of $297,000. Two weeks later in Orlando, Florida, he won again.

By 1997, Tiger was roaring. He became the first minority golfer to win the famed Masters Tournament. Fifty million TV viewers watched him calmly sink a five-foot putt. His final score broke the record set by Jack Nicklaus, the great golfer of the 1960s and 1970s. Cheers rang out

Wearing his lucky red shirt, Tiger pumps his fist after winning his very first major and his first Masters in 1997.

as Tiger greeted his parents. Tiger buried his head in his dad's shoulders and wept with joy. Then he hugged his mom and cried some more.

Tiger works with kids at one of his foundation's golf clinics.

Tiger has used his success to help others. The Tiger Woods Foundation holds golf clinics throughout the country. At the clinics, kids get advice about golf and practice their driving and putting skills. The foundation also runs programs that encourage kids to be healthy and to stay in school.

Meanwhile, Tiger hasn't stopped winning. He captured the Masters title again in 2001 and 2002. He has also won other majors, such as the U.S. Open, the British Open, and the PGA Championship. He has won more pro tournaments at his age than anyone else—ever.

Tiger held the lead in the final round of the 2002 U.S. Open and won the tournament. Here he kisses the trophy.

Tiger has often been compared to Jack Nicklaus. Tiger and Jack *(second from right)* played against Lee Trevino and Sergio Garcia in the **prime time** Battle at Bighorn in 2002.

Before Tiger came along, many considered Jack Nicklaus to be the greatest golfer to ever live. When Tiger was ten years old, he tacked a piece of paper onto his wall. It was a list of golf records that Nicklaus held. Tiger stared at the list each day. His goal was to break those records someday. That time has come. Tiger breaks more and more records each year. The way he is going, we may soon be calling Tiger Woods the greatest golfer to ever live.

Selected Career Highlights

2002 Won Masters Tournament for the third time
Won U.S. Open for the second time

2001 Won Masters Tournament for the second time
Was reigning champion of all four majors at the same time
Named PGA Player of the Year for the fourth time
Received ESPY award as Outstanding Male Athlete of the Year

2000 Won U.S. Open, British Open, PGA Championship
Named Male Athlete of the Year by the *Associated Press* and
PGA Player of the Year, both for the third time
Named *Sports Illustrated* Sportsman of the Year and received
ESPY award as Outstanding Male Athlete of the Year, both
for the second time

1999 Won PGA Championship
Again named Male Athlete of the Year by *Associated Press*
and PGA Player of the Year

1998 Received ESPY award as Outstanding Male Athlete of the Year

1997 Won Masters Tournament for the first time
Named Male Athlete of the Year by *Associated Press* and PGA
Player of the Year

1996 Left Stanford and turned pro
Won first PGA Tour event, Las Vegas Invitational
Named *Sports Illustrated* Sportsman of the Year

1994–1996 While at Stanford University, won U.S. Amateur
Championship three years in a row

1991–1993 Won U.S. Junior Amateur Tournament three years
in a row

1987 Won all thirty junior tournaments entered

1984 Won first junior world tournament

GLOSSARY

amateur: an athlete who receives no prize money for playing in an event

driver: the biggest, most powerful club in a golfer's bag

driving range: an area where golfers practice hitting golf balls

endorsement: approval of a product in public to help sell it

fairway: on a golf course, the long, grassy area that stretches from the tee (where the ball is first struck) to the green (where the hole is)

green: on a golf course, the small, grassy area where the hole (cup) is

hole in one: when the ball is hit off the tee and lands in the hole using only one stroke

major: one of four international golf tournaments held each year. The tournaments are the Masters, the U.S. Open, the British Open, and the PGA Championship.

miss the cut: to be taken out of competition in a tournament because of having a score that is too high. The score, or cut, is set after players play two (of four) rounds of golf. Players must "make the cut" to get to play the final two rounds.

par: the number of strokes from tee to green a player is supposed to need to get the ball in the hole. One stroke less than par is called a birdie. One stroke more is called a bogey.

prime time: the evening hours, when the largest group of people will be watching television

prize money: the money awarded to each player, based on his or her finishing score

professional: a player who receives money for playing in an event

Professional Golfers' Association (PGA): the group that oversees the tournaments in which professional male golfers play

putt: to tap the ball gently so it will go in the hole on the green

putting green: a grassy area where golfers practice putting

stroke: hitting the golf ball with a club. Also called a shot

tee up: to set up the golf ball on a peg (the tee) before striking it

FURTHER READING & WEBSITES

Emerson, Carl. *Tiger Woods*. Chanhassen, MN: The Child's World, 2000.

Gutelle, Andrew. *Tiger Woods*. New York: Grosset & Dunlap, 2002.

Hughes, Libby. *Tiger Woods: A Biography for Kids*. Columbus, MS: Genesis Press, Inc., 2000.

Krause, Peter. *Play-By-Play Golf*. Minneapolis: LernerSports, 2002.

MacNow, Glen. *Tiger Woods*. Berkeley Heights, NJ: Enslow Publishers, Inc., 2001.

Stewart, Mark. *Tiger Woods: Drive to Greatness*. Brookfield, CT: Millbrook Press, 2001.

Williams, Jean Kinney. *Tiger Woods: Professional Golfer*. Chicago: Ferguson Publishing, 2001.

Woods, Earl. *Start Something: You Can Make a Difference*. New York: Simon & Schuster, 2000.

PGA Tour
<http://www.pgatour.com>
A website developed by the Professional Golfers' Association (PGA) that provides fans with recent news stories, biographies of golfers, and information about tournaments

Sports Illustrated for Kids
<http://www.sikids.com>
The *Sports Illustrated for Kids* website that covers all sports, including golf

Tiger's Website
<http://www.tigerwoods.com>
Tiger's official website, featuring trivia, photos, and information about golf

The Tiger Woods Foundation
<http://www.twfound.org>
The official website of Tiger's foundation, which runs junior golf clinics and educational programs around the country

INDEX

PHOTO ACKNOWLEDGMENTS

Photographs are used with the permission of: © Robert Beck/SI/Icon SMI, p. 4; AP/Wide World Photos, p. 6; © Craig Jones/Getty Images, pp. 7, 23, 29; © David Strick/CORBIS OUTLINE, pp. 8, 10; San Diego Union-Tribune/Dave Siccardi, p. 11; © Ken Levine/Getty Images, p. 12; © Duomo/CORBIS, pp. 13, 14; © Gary Newkirk/Getty Images, p. 16; © Rusty Jarrett/Getty Images, p. 18; © David Cannon/Getty Images, p. 20; © J.D. Cuban/Getty Images, p. 21; © Jamie Squire/Getty Images, p. 22; © Stephen Mundy/Getty Images, p. 25; © Reuters NewMedia, Inc./CORBIS, p. 26; © Donald Miralle/Getty Images, p. 27; © Scott Halleran/Getty Images, p. 28.

Cover: © Scott Halleran/Getty Images.